Confident Reader titles are ideal for greater reading confidence and stami read simple stories with a wider vocabulary.

Special features:

Wider vocabulary, reinforced through repetition

Detailed pictures for added interest and discussion

Captions and labels clarify information

Longer sentences

Ladybird

Educational Consultants: Geraldine Taylor and James Clements
Book Banding Consultant: Kate Ruttle
Subject Consultant: Philip Parker

LADYBIRD BOOKS
UK | USA | Canada | Ireland | Australia
India | New Zealand | South Africa

Ladybird Books is part of the Penguin Random House group of companies
whose addresses can be found at global.penguinrandomhouse.com.

www.penguin.co.uk   www.puffin.co.uk   www.ladybird.co.uk

First published 2018
This edition published 2024
001

Written by Chris Baker
Text copyright © Ladybird Books Ltd, 2018, 2024
Illustrations by Ruby Taylor
Illustrations copyright © Ladybird Books Ltd, 2018, 2024

The moral right of the author and illustrator has been asserted

Printed in China

The authorized representative in the EEA is Penguin Random House Ireland,
Morrison Chambers, 32 Nassau Street, Dublin D02 YH68

A CIP catalogue record for this book is available from the British Library

ISBN: 978-0-241-56366-3

All correspondence to:
Ladybird Books
Penguin Random House Children's
One Embassy Gardens, 8 Viaduct Gardens, London SW11 7BW

Ancient Egypt

Written by Chris Baker
Illustrated by Ruby Taylor

Contents

Ancient Egypt	8
Pharaohs	10
The River Nile	12
Floods and mud	14
Using floods	16
Life on the River Nile	18
Life in ancient Egypt	20
Egyptian writing	22
Time to play	24
Gods and the afterlife	26
The afterlife	28
Mummies	30
How to make a mummy	32
Time for the afterlife	34
Tombs	36
Tutankhamun's tomb	38

The pyramid tomb	40
Ancient Egypt today	42
Picture glossary	44
Index	46
Ancient Egypt quiz	47

Ancient Egypt

The ancient Egyptians lived many years in the past. They had rulers who were very powerful.

4500–3600 BCE
People first live by the River Nile.

2650 BCE
The first pyramid is made.

3200 BCE
People first use hieroglyphic writing.

2551–2528 BCE
Khufu rules Egypt.

1333–1324 BCE
Tutankhamun rules Egypt.

51–30 BCE
Cleopatra rules Egypt.

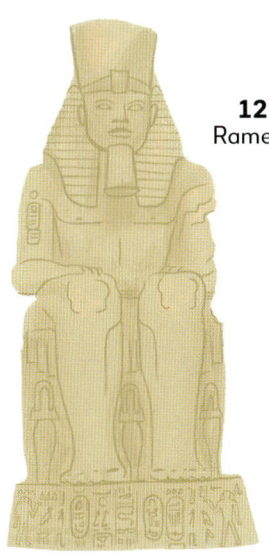

1290–1224 BCE
Rameses II rules Egypt.

Pharaohs

The ruler of the ancient Egyptians was the pharaoh. The people thought the pharaoh was like a god.

Powerful pharaohs

Khufu made a pyramid.

Rameses II made lots of buildings.

Tutankhamun was a boy ruler.

Cleopatra ruled for 21 years.

The River Nile

The ancient Egyptians lived by the River Nile. They took water from the river and learned how to use it to grow food.

Egypt today

Africa

Floods and mud

In the past, the River Nile flooded every year.

plants for food

Using floods

The ancient Egyptians learned when the River Nile was going to flood. Then, they could plant at the right time.

water from the River Nile

They could look here to see where the flood was going to be.

Life on the River Nile
The ancient Egyptians had lots of food and water because of the river.

Look at the many things that used the river.

Life in ancient Egypt

The ancient Egyptians could grow and make good food with the help of the river.

Egyptian writing

Ancient Egyptians learned reading and writing. They used hieroglyphics, which was like writing with pictures.

hieroglyphics

tomb

People know a lot about ancient Egyptian life by reading their hieroglyphic writing.

Time to play

Ancient Egyptians had time to play. People can see this from their writing, and from things in their tombs.

25

Gods and the afterlife

The ancient Egyptians thought there were lots of gods. They thought the gods could help them in life, and when they were dead.

Here are some ancient Egyptian gods.

The afterlife

Ancient Egyptians thought that if they were good they would go to the afterlife when they died.

soul   gods

They thought the gods would know if a soul was good, and if it could go to the afterlife.

Ancient Egyptians thought this god took the souls of people who were not good.

Mummies

Ancient Egyptians thought that people's souls could come back to their dead body.

They made a mummy to preserve the body for the soul.

The ancient Egyptians thought this god helped to make mummies.

How to make a mummy

The ancient Egyptians took the insides from the dead body, and put them in jars. Then, they preserved the body with salt.

dead body

salt to preserve the body

Time for the afterlife

The ancient Egyptians put bandages around the body. They put it in a tomb with things for the soul to use in the afterlife.

This is how they put bandages around the body.

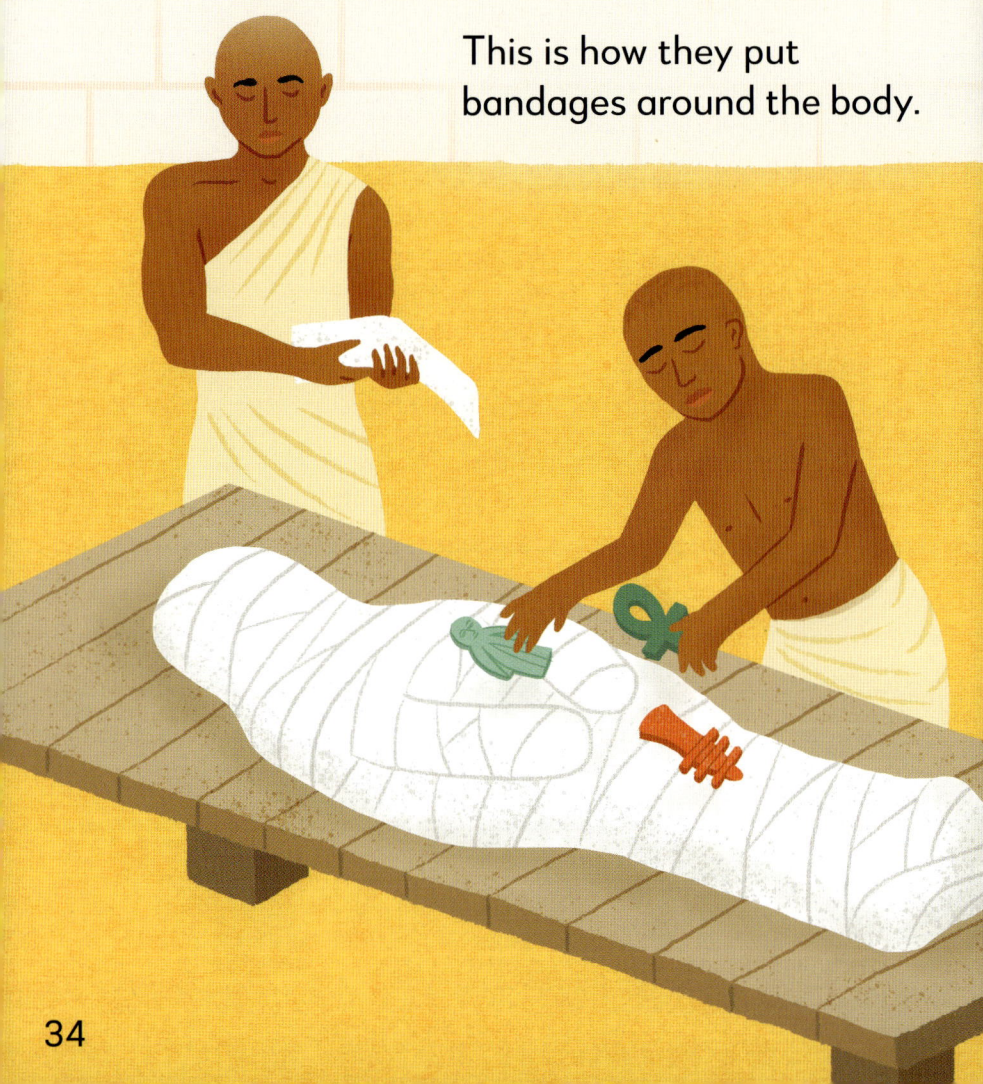

Tombs

The ancient Egyptians put models and pictures in the tomb with the mummy.

pictures

They thought that in the afterlife these would be used by the soul.

Tutankhamun's tomb

The pharaohs had beautiful tombs. The boy pharaoh, Tutankhamun, had very beautiful things to use in the afterlife!

Tutankhamun

This is Tutankhamun's tomb.

The pyramid tomb

Some tombs were pyramids.

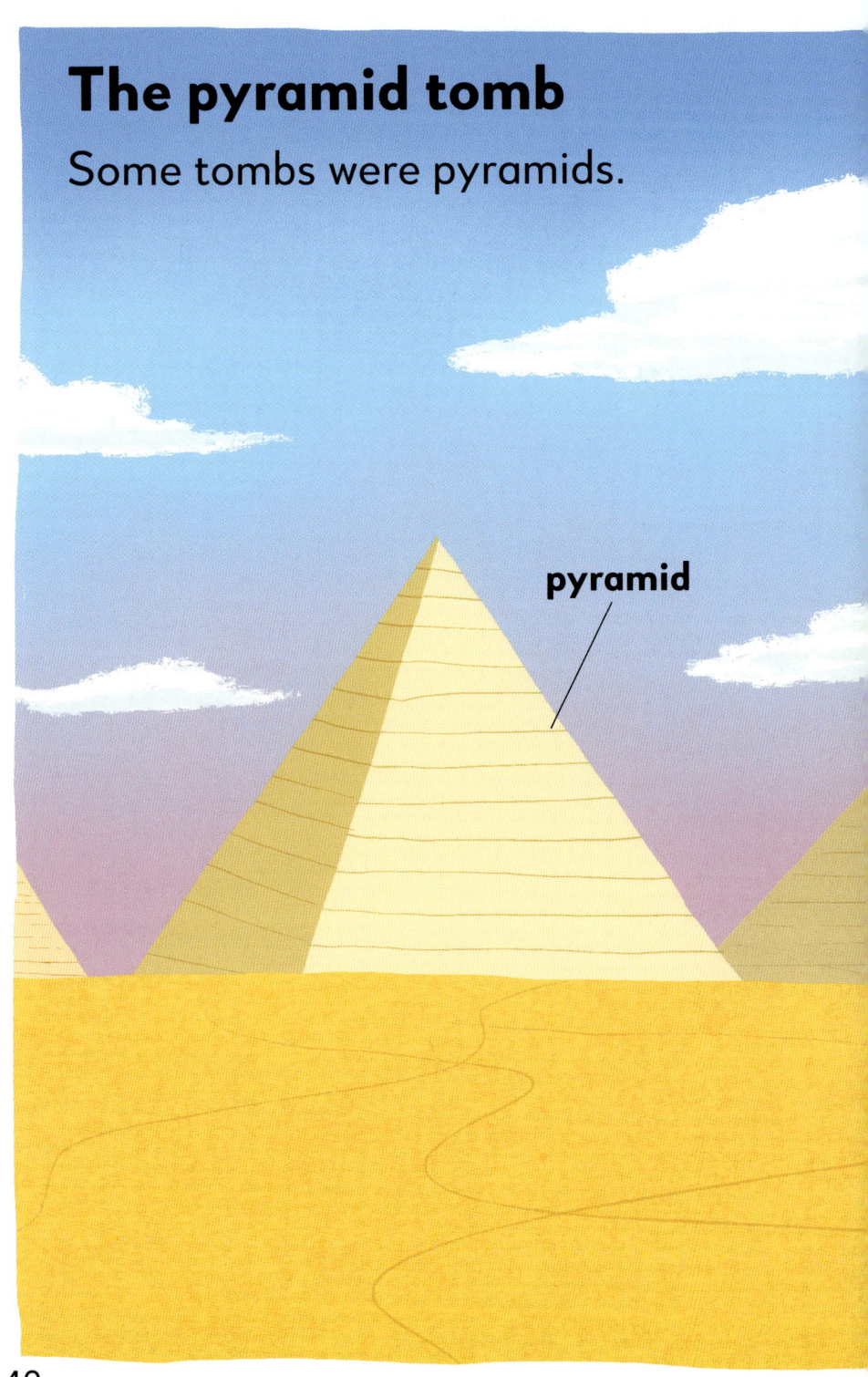

Building a pyramid took a lot of time!

These ancient Egyptians are building Pharaoh Khufu's pyramid.

Ancient Egypt today

People can go and see the pyramids today, or see lots of ancient Egyptian things in a museum.

a pyramid today

There are lots of ancient Egyptian things at this museum.

Picture glossary

 Cleopatra

 Egypt today

 flood

 gods

 hieroglyphics

 Khufu